Oxford Studies of Composers (19)

LAS

JEROME ROCHE

London

OXFORD UNIVERSITY PRESS

NEW YORK   MELBOURNE

1982

Oxford University Press, Walton Street, Oxford OX2 6DP

London Glasgow New York Toronto
Delhi Bombay Calcutta Madras Karachi
Kuala Lumpur Singapore Hong Kong Tokyo
Nairobi Dar es Salaam Cape Town
Melbourne Auckland

and associates in
Beirut Berlin Ibadan Mexico City Nicosia

ISBN 0 19 315237 1

British Library Cataloguing in Publication Data

Roche, Jerome
Lassus. – (Oxford studies of composers; 19)
I. Title
780'.92   ML410.L3
ISBN 0-19-315237-1

*Printed in Great Britain
at the University Press, Oxford
by Eric Buckley
Printer to the University*

CONTENTS

INTRODUCTION

LASSUS has for some time been regarded as one of the great masters of the art of polyphony working in the autumn of the Renaissance, and a substantial scholarly edition of his works was undertaken by German editors at the turn of the century, not long after that of Palestrina's works. Yet, perhaps precisely because Lassus chose to spend by far the greater part of his life in Germany, the bulk of writing about his life and music has been in German, with comparatively little available to English readers apart from the necessarily brief surveys in standard textbooks. The object of this modest study is to go a little way towards filling that gap, giving a more or less chronological view of Lassus's activities within each of the many genres he cultivated, and reflecting the sheer vastness and variety of his output by drawing attention to a reasonably broad sampling of his works without, it is hoped, falling prey to mere list-making.

The composer's name is written as inconsistently today as it was in his own time. To the argument that Lassus (English usage) is preferable to Lasso (American and German) since the latter requires its preposition 'di', one may counter that the majority of the composer's surviving letters were signed 'Orlando Lasso'. We shall nevertheless stick to Orlandus Lassus (Latin) rather than the Italian form or indeed the French Roland de Lassus, which was not used in the France of his day, where he was known as 'Orlande'.

Orlandus Lassus, then, was born at Mons, now in Walloon Belgium, most probably in 1532, and as a choirboy there was involved in music from his earliest years. On account of his beautiful voice he was twice abducted abroad; when this happened a third time he stayed of his own free will and joined the service of the Viceroy of Sicily at the age of twelve.[1] During the ensuing ten years in Italy (1544–54) he visited other Spanish dependencies such as Milan and Naples and later went to Rome in 1551 to become choirmaster at St. John Lateran (his successor was Palestrina, but the two may never have met). In 1554 he

---

[1] Some commentators have suggested that these kidnappings were romanticized myth; Leuchtmann in his recent authoritative biography *Orlando di Lasso: sein Leben* (Wiesbaden, 1976) accepts their veracity.

returned north to Antwerp to supervise his first publications, and may have visited England in Philip II's retinue. By his mid-twenties Lassus had seen the world, in a succession of aristocratic, priestly, and bourgeois environments, and had published sixty compositions, maybe a third of his output to date.

It was no nonentity, therefore, that Duke Albrecht V of Bavaria took into his service as singer at his court chapel at Munich in 1557, and appointed Kapellmeister in 1562 after the ailing Ludwig Daser's voluntary retirement. And it was in that position that Lassus remained for the rest of his life. The early years at Munich were ones of indefatigable industry: it is an amazing fact that Lassus wrote almost a third of his whole output in the period 1560–7. Yet he often travelled within Germany on his duties, and went abroad to engage new musicians and disseminate his music — to Venice several times, to France, The Netherlands, and in 1574 to Rome to receive a great honour from Pope Gregory XIII, the Knighthood of the Golden Spur. The Venice visits brought him into contact with the Gabrielis, and in 1574 he may have brought the young Giovanni to Munich: certainly the latter stayed at the Bavarian court for several years, imbibing the opulence of the internationally star-studded musical establishment. Lassus could act, too: in 1568 he took the part of Magnifico in a *commedia dell'arte* entertainment at the marriage of Duke Wilhelm with Renée of Lorraine, an experience reflected in some of his lighter Italian secular music and also in the frothy humour of his letters to the young Duke, who became a bosom friend. In their comic mixture of languages, these letters were characteristic of a man who could set so many to music with equal fluency.

Even as early as 1566 Lassus was distinguished enough in his adopted home to achieve an entry in a reference work by Samuel Quickelberg, humanist writer at the Munich court: a youthful fame perhaps comparable only with Mozart's in his day. Later in life, he could surely have had any coveted post for the asking, but by 1580 he felt too old to accept invitations even as tempting as that to succeed Scandello at the Dresden court. This is surprising, because in 1579 Duke Albrecht had died leaving a mountain of debts, and it was clear that his successor Wilhelm would be forced to make savage cuts in the accustomed musical splendours, as indeed happened. Moreover, Wilhelm was a staunch advocate of Counter-Reformation tendencies towards a more rigorous religious life, introducing Jesuits to the court and discouraging the festive and convivial atmosphere of earlier years. All this told on Lassus, who was naturally given to melancholy:

combined with the overwork involved in producing a sudden torrent of new music in the early 1580s, nervous exhaustion and depression took its toll, and economic worries about the future of his wife and sons did not help. His comparatively unproductive last years ended with his death in June 1594.

'Unproductive', however, hardly seems a word appropriate to any part of Lassus's life. Leuchtmann[2] has estimated that between 1555 and his death there appeared 530 publications containing at least something by Lassus – more than one a month! – and that this represents about half of all the music printed in those years: staggering figures indeed.

[2] Leuchtmann, op. cit., p. 44.

THE MOTETS

PRIDE of place in Lassus's sacred output must go to the motets, just as in Palestrina's it goes to the Masses. There are no less than some 530 in all: the majority (almost two-thirds) are for five or six voices, while only one-fifth are for four voices, and there are small numbers respectively for seven voices upwards, or for just two or three – the little *bicinia* or *tricinia* as Lassus's contemporaries would have known them. These statistics are perhaps surprising, and not proportionate to our present-day appreciation of Lassus's motets, which has tended to favour the smaller textures — four-part and less — for reasons of practicality in performance or the study of counterpoint, so it will be the task of this chapter to redress the balance by giving due weight to the more solidly written works that represent the core of Lassus's motet style and illustrate his prodigious contrapuntal technique.

Two important works, the Penitential Psalms and the *Prophetiae Sibyllarum*, are commonly grouped under the generic heading 'motets', and indeed belong in the present chapter rather than elsewhere; but they are each unique in their way, and will therefore be treated separately at the end rather than in the generally chronological survey that follows shortly. On the other hand, all music designated for precise liturgical occasions — Masses, Canticles, Offices, Lamentations, and so on — will be considered in the chapters on 'Other Liturgical Works' and 'The Madrigals and Villanellas'. A true appreciation of Lassus's motets has long been hampered by the fact that the old series (*alte Reihe*) of the collected edition follows the arrangement of the huge posthumous *Magnum opus musicum* brought out in 1604 by Lassus's sons. Here, grouping the motets according to vocal scoring completely obscured their chronology, while the printing of many with substitute texts even created problems of identification. Boetticher's monumental work on Lassus[1] sought to disentangle the resultant confusion by assigning the motets, where possible, to their original publications and surveying the music in large-scale chronological phases. These phases are used as a guide in the present study, though they must not be regarded as entirely

---

[1] W. Boetticher, *Orlando di Lasso und sein Zeit, 1532–1594* (Kassel, 1958).

satisfactory or conclusive; they are useful in so far as they provide a framework for some kind of orientation, and relate works to published collections, even though these can never provide an infallible aid to dating.

Another point that remains to be made is that Lassus's motets, unlike those of Palestrina, Byrd, or Victoria, are by no means exclusively religious. Four distinct non-religious headings need to be borne in mind: (*a*) didactic motets, largely consisting of two- and three-part pieces with moralistic rather than liturgical texts. This was music for study and practice, to be used by the students of Lassus and his followers, and still ideal today for the demonstration of contrapuntal techniques; (*b*) ceremonial or homage motets, written in honour of a particular patron or for a particular occasion such as a state visit; (*c*) motets with classical texts by such writers as Virgil or Horace: Lassus was one of a line of Renaissance composers to set the lament of Dido, *Dulces exuviae*; and (*d*) humorous motets, to texts in praise of wine, for example, or which paint words in a manner extravagant enough to be quite out of place in church. This leaves the vast corpus of religious motets, and even this contains some sub-categories: Marian antiphons, settings of Mass Propers, Gospels, Epistles, isolated psalm verses, complete psalms. Here the difficulty lies in assigning many of these to any precise liturgical context. One may with some confidence assume that Marian antiphon settings were not only used as motets and for devotional purposes, but also to conclude the choral Office at Munich. It may also be asked whether the complete psalms might have been used for the Office, for which reason they will be considered later as a separate entity.

Lassus's early years saw two publications with motets, his 1555 *opus primum* (a mixture of four-part music, including also chansons, madrigals, and villanellas), and the important five- and six-part collection of 1556; both were issued at Antwerp during his stay there between periods in Rome and Munich. The little motets of 1555 show the effects of his Italian musical upbringing, whether in the lucid, exquisite scoring of a piece like *Peccantem me quotidie* or in the bold chromaticism of *Alma nemes*, in which Lassus owed a specific debt to Rore. The so-called 'Antwerp motet book' of 1556 reveals how thoroughly Lassus familiarized himself with Netherlandish music, with its composers, musicians, and publishers; with the fully matured style of the *ars perfecta* of Josquin des Prez and his followers Gombert and Clemens non Papa. The stage had already been set for the motet to become the dominant genre of sacred music, but around 1550 there was, as Lowinsky argues,[2] a change of motet style reflecting a change of concept: away from a purely religious idea towards that of man and his world capturing the limelight — humanism, in fact. Music became related to drama through rhetoric, an art that underlies many of Lassus's motets. A smooth flow would be interrupted by pauses and dramatic exclamations, and the music would take on a 'speaking' quality. This can be seen in the slow, majestic chordal sonorities of *Tibi laus*, a paean to the Trinity, which reduce from five to just three voices at the mention of that very word:

Ex. 1

Clearly, however, Lassus owed something to his predecessors: to Gombert, 'a plastic and expressive value'[3] in the motet themes, and to Clemens, the use of a symbolic *ostinato*; he adapted the latter's *Fremuit spiritu Jesus* as a 'parody motet', extending the *ostinato* that carries the words 'Lazare veni foras' ('Lazarus come forth') in a bold treatment of the raising of Lazarus from the dead. The Antwerp motet book contains a sizeable proportion of homage motets whose existence is explicable only by reference to their texts. *Te spectant Reginalde Poli* is addressed to the English Cardinal Pole, whom Lassus may have met in Rome. 'The stars smile at you, the mountains exult', says the text, and the composer responds with a rash of crotchet *melisma* and a sharply profiled motive; at the mention of 'England', there is clear homophony; but perhaps most audible musically is the notable increase in accidentals as the motet nears its end — many B flats, F and C sharps colour the G mode, introduce a 'delayed chromaticism' into the final point, and make the end seem like a Picardy third:

[2] E. Lowinsky, *Secret Chromatic Art in the Netherlands Motet* (New York, 1946), p. 21.
[3] N. Bridgman: 'Latin Church Music on the Continent - 1', *The New Oxford History of Music*, iv (London, 1968), p. 219.

This same harmonic feature also occurs at the end of *Mirabile mysterium* in the same mode, a motet of visionary spirituality which expounds the mystery of the incarnation in solid, rolling, imitative counterpoint. This manner, which eschews homophony but preserves contrasts of *chiaroscuro* through economic use of the five parts, recalls Gombert. But, as often, Lassus has a surprise at the end, for suddenly the top part breaks into very long notes, with festoons of *melisma* below — a visual notational symbol for the words 'neque divisionem', best appreciated as originally printed:

Ex. 3

The first ten of Lassus's Munich years may be taken as the next phase of his creative life, up to about 1567. The first motet book of these German years was the *Sacrae cantiones* issued at Nuremberg in 1562. This was so popular that it was reprinted no less than twenty times in Germany and Italy. Fame indeed, and no wonder, for it contains some of his finest five-part motets: festal pieces for major church festivals rather than the occasional ones of the Antwerp book, or settings of meditative texts drawn from the psalms. *Surgens Jesus*, for Easter, opens with a sinuous idea whose angularity contrasts well with one of Palestrina's treatments of the same word, worked in imitative entries; but it is often the rhythmic excitement and sheer command of sonority as much as the contrapuntal working that amaze, especially since all five voices are active throughout. Lassus's deft control of pace and harmonic movement, learned as a madrigalist, ensure that such textures are never monotonous. The striking opening idea is even more evident in the Epiphany motet *Videntes stellam*:

4

Vi-dentes stel - lam Ma - gi ga-vi -si · sunt,

whose brilliant textures owe much to the use of two high top parts of equal range. In complete contrast stands *In me transierunt*, a sombre motet that was subjected to rhetorical analysis in Burmeister's *Musica poetica* of 1606.[4] This writer compares a motet to a classically ordered speech with its *exordium*, *confirmatio*, and *epilogus* corresponding to the opening point, the body of the piece, and the peroration respectively. In its modality, this work affords an example of how the Phrygian became increasingly indistinct from the Aeolian, or modern A minor mode.

Lassus's early fame ensured his being represented in great anthologies of motets like the 1564 *Thesaurus musicus* of his Nuremberg publishers. To this he contributed the famous six-part *Timor et tremor* whose amazing chromatic harmonies are brought about by both chromatic alterations and false relations, but whose brevity is, in Haar's opinion,[5] equally surprising. Another contribution, illustrating Lassus's sense of structure, was the four-part *Quasi cedrus*. In this a pure arch form can be observed: of the seven sections, the second and sixth alternate duo writing between upper and lower pairs of voices, and the third and fifth use block chords in triple time, with shifting cross-accents. This is how the second leads into the third, in which textual stress marks indicate the cross-rhythms:

[4] Burmeister's theories are expounded in C. Palisca, 'Ut oratoria musica', *The Meaning of Mannerism* (Hanover, N.H., 1972). The comparison between music and rhetoric yields interesting and historically valid avenues of research into musical analysis, though it has yet to be applied at all widely in the late Renaissance repertory. Certainly it comes to mind repeatedly in the case of much of Lassus's music, as the ensuing pages will show.

[5] J. Haar, 'Lassus', *The New Grove Dictionary of Music and Musicians* (London, 1980). I am grateful to Professor Haar for allowing me to read his article before publication.

Ex. 5

That Lassus's reputation was spreading in France is evidenced by the publication of two motet books in Paris in 1564 and 1565, the first of which was dedicated to an adviser of the French king. This contains the moving setting of words from Ecclesiasticus, *O mors quam amara est* for six voices, reflective in tone and cautious in word painting. From the second Paris book comes the well-known *Tristis est anima mea*, a good illustration of the fact that sadness and the major mode are not incompatible: Lassus achieves his effects through colour and drooping melodic lines, as at 'vos fugam' with its grinding passing-note dissonances. This quotation (Ex. 6) begins with one of Lassus's typical side-stepping V–IV cadences, as well as showing his feel for chord spacing:

Ex. 6

Missus est Gabriel is a Gospel motet, setting the complete narrative of the annunciation (Luke 1: 26–38) in four sections. While there is no attempt to represent the angel and the Virgin by specific groups of voices in dialogue fashion, the long text comes over with some immediacy. The textures vary from the pellucid, Josquin-like sparseness of the opening to the solid homophony of 'ecce ancilla Domini' at the end, and the whole third section is for three out of the five voices.

The mode is Phrygian. Notice the wonderful chord change for 'ecce concipies':

Ex. 7

As well as Gospel readings, certain strophic Office hymn texts inspired Lassus at this time, though the fact that they are not built on plainsong (unlike Palestrina's and Victoria's hymns) excludes them from strict liturgical performance. The motet book which Scotto issued in Venice in 1565 has the six-part *Vexilla regis*, a celebrated Passiontide motet, while an anthology he issued in 1567 has the fine but lesser known *Jesu nostra redemptio*. The scoring of this piece is weighted towards low voices (SAATBB) and, like *Missus est Gabriel*, the work falls into four sections of which the third reduces the texture, in this case to just two voices. The final section is striking for its use of short, balanced phrases passed between the voice-groups in quasi-polychoral manner, following the poetic caesuras of the text. For a true double-choir work assignable to the 1560s there is no better example than *Tui sunt caeli*, a setting of the Christmas Day Offertory. 'Thine are the heavens and thine the earth': no surprise that Lassus should distinguish the two realms by contrasting phrases for a high choir and a normal-pitch one. But this motet well illustrates Lassus's preference for brilliant, rich tutti effects, without much of the varied phrasing and rapid-fire dialogue of the Venetians. Where this does occur, however, the different pitches of the two choirs are exploited to give 'harmonic' as well as spatial responses.[6]

Let us now move on to the years of Lassus's early maturity, from 1568 to 1573 or so. These saw the absolute peak of his motet production and publication, with the appearance in six years of no less than twenty-four collections, a rate not even Palestrina could achieve.[7] Of the German prints, we may mention the Nuremberg *Selectissimae*

[6] For further discussion of Lassus's double-choir music, see D. Arnold, 'The Grand Motets of Orlandus Lassus', *Early Music*, vi (1978), pp. 170–81.

[7] Boetticher, op. cit., p. 358.

cantiones (1568) in two volumes, one including the Passiontide motet *In monte Oliveti* for SAATBB (sombre scoring again); and the Munich five-part *Cantiones* of the following year, which includes the delightful *Resonet*. Rarely for Lassus, he refers to the popular Christmas carol melody in the opening passage. The work is given a satisfying shape with the middle one of the three sections a *tricinium*, and the outer ones both concluding with joyous cries of 'Eja! Virgo Deum genuit' in almost bucolic triple time. This unreservedly joyous mood is shared by non-religious, convivial motets like *Vinum bonum*, a double-choir dialogue that Lassus appended to a Munich motet book of 1570. Such a piece, in praise of wine, would doubtless have graced a festive social occasion at the court.

Outside Germany, Louvain and Paris were the main outlets for Lassus's copious motet production at this time. The Louvain book of four-part pieces (1569) contains a fine setting of the short lesson for Compline, *Fratres sobrii*, full of sharply-etched motives for each phrase of text. The *exordium* of classical speech is unmistakable in the opening call to attention: 'Brethren! (be sober and watchful)':

Ex. 8

No less striking are the insistent rhythms and sequences of 'resistite' ('whom resist ye, strong in faith') later on. But perhaps Lassus's rhetorical best can be observed in *Stabunt justi*, a five-part Epistle motet from the Paris collection of 1571, brought out to keep him in vogue with the French musical public. The noble text, from the Book of Wisdom, forms the Epistle for Mass of a martyr; the musical setting catches its every nuance with a plainly audible 'figure'. In the following extract the words mean 'these [the wicked] seeing it shall be troubled with terrible fear, and shall be amazed at the suddenness of their [the just men] unexpected salvation':

Ex. 9

The nervous rhythmic tension and rapid declamation are particularly notable here, as later in the motet; by contrast, the peroration 'their lot is among the saints' is a confident paragraph of wonderfully rolling counterpoint:

Ex. 10

Here indeed is the quintessential Lassus.

Boetticher views the years 1573-9 as the phase of 'representative art' in the composer's career. His domination of the German musical scene is reflected in the strong influence he now wielded over the court composers, and his position of honour in Munich by the publication there of five luxury volumes of his sacred music, the *Patrocinium musices* (1573-6), at the instigation of Duke Wilhelm. At the same time his cosmopolitanism is evidenced by the multilingual collection issued at Munich in 1573, Latin motets jostling with madrigals, chansons, and lieder: one can detect a trace of secular influence in the moral motet *Fallax gratia*, with its numerous decorated, melismatic musical shapes. Non-religious motets of secular inspiration often appeared in mainly secular publications, like the humorous *Bestia curvafia pulices*, included in a chanson book of 1576. This hilarious doggerel is set in the chordal style of the French *musique mesurée*, with clear attention to poetic accents—a Latin chanson indeed, and a hybrid bred of Lassus's international outlook. At the other extreme stand works which exude the serious intense spirit of the Counter-Reformation that began to overshadow Munich court life, like the *Lauda Sion* and the setting of the Athanasian Creed (published in the Paris *Moduli* of 1577). The text of the first of these, the sequence for Mass of Corpus Christi, has earnest dogmatic overtones in tune with this spirit, and the feast itself was a high point in the Munich liturgical calendar. Lassus's setting falls into four extended sections of about a hundred bars each, and draws freely upon the plainsong melody as well as presenting it as a tenor *cantus firmus*—a severely traditional treatment not common in his motets.

The year 1577 was a good one for an aspiring student of music, whether a pupil of Lassus himself or of one of his followers, since it saw publication at Munich of a volume each of two- and three-part motets whose purpose was primarily didactic. Their validity as a model for contrapuntal studies is scarcely less today in those institutions that still value such a discipline: their sheer resourcefulness makes a contrast with the greater austerity and formalism of Palestrina's *tricinia* (Palestrina, of course, wrote no two-part music). One notices especially the variety of melodic intervals of imitation — the second and seventh are as common as the fourth or fifth — and the felicitous sense of musical climax even in such miniatures. The severe, modal counterpoint, far removed from Lassus's rhetorical manner and rooted firmly in the Franco-Flemish tradition of earlier decades, is well illustrated in *Cantate Domino* or *Domine Deus meus* for three voices. Quite different *tricinia* can be found in the posthumous *Magnum opus musicum*: these are for three equal voices, and exploit delicate triadic sonorities with interweaving imitation at the unison, as *Agimus tibi gratias* shows:

Ex. 11

Such music is ideal for choirs of high voices, and is deservedly popular today.

Other pieces from this posthumous collection assignable to the 1570s include the humorous *In hora ultima*, a kind of Renaissance 'Surprise Symphony' with vividly extravagant musical figures for the words 'trumpet, pipe, and lyre, joking, laughing, jumping, and singing' which belie the slow, solemn opening; and two excellent Marian antiphons, a four-part *Salve Regina* (II) and a six-part *Alma Redemptoris* (II). The first of these is an excellent illustration of Lassus's nervous style, exhibited in rapid harmonic change, chains of suspensions, and thwarted cadences (note his beloved V-IV at 'flentes'):

Ex. 12

The other revels in subtle variations of scoring, declaiming the words in a kind of decorated homophony that has something in common with Palestrina's later six-part music. An especially fine work is *Domine Jesu Christe* in five parts, whose text is a paraphrase of Psalm 50: where the opening words of that psalm occur at the end of the *prima pars*, Lassus cannot resist quoting the motto that Josquin had used in his *Miserere* many years before. This music has a spaciousness not often encountered in his late motets. The two ideas of 'averte Domine faciem tuam' are expounded in no less than twenty-four bars, whose technical brilliance can be judged from the following short extract:

Ex. 13

The years from 1580 onwards can be viewed as Lassus's late phase. Before ill-health took its toll, the early 1580s saw a new wave of motet publication in Germany, particularly in 1582 and 1585. The six-part *Mottetta* issued at Munich in 1582 is notable for his *Ave verum*, a motet of textural contrasts, again, and occasional bitter-sweet false relations. The final plea for mercy is most moving, with its stark

'Amen', and Lassus invents a characteristic drooping figure for 'in cruce pro homine'. The very same type of figure turns up in a passage from the motet *Justorum animae*, in the second voice:

Ex. 14

This inspiring work ends with a marvellous 'harmonic rallentando' at the words 'they are in peace', with just three changes of harmony in the final eight bars. It appeared in a five-part Munich motet book of the same year, along with the fine Easter motet *Christus resurgens*, whose conciseness of utterance and terseness of musical material are absolutely typical of late Lassus.

These features tended to dominate his music most in his handling of the four-part texture, as we can see in the works of the 1585 Munich *Sacrae cantiones*. Many of these are no more than forty bars or so in length, and though on the whole they avoid pure block chordal writing, their openings are never spaciously 'fugal', as in many of Palestrina's four-part motets, but rather tend to be compressed in such a way that all four voices enter rapidly. Pair imitation, as in *Benedic anima mea* or the well-known *Jubilate Deo*, is a long-hallowed device; more modern are the 'modulating' sequences that provide a musical climax to both these motets, not so much for being sequences (which Josquin had used long ago) as for providing rapid modal excursions in order to lend some finality to the concluding cadence. It is a remarkable fact that this conciseness does not preclude a modicum of development for each musical figure prompted by the successive word-groups. For instance, the text of one motet is divided up thus: 'Domine / labia mea aperies / et os meum / annuntiabit / laudem tuam'. Not much less than half the motet is given to the final phrase, but nearly all the others are sung more than once in a continuously unfolding argument — all this in just thirty-seven bars. Lassus's liking for angular lines is evident. A study of leaps reveals the bass to be the most angular, as we would expect, but the upper voices are sometimes not much less so. As for the texts of these short motets, many of them consist of isolated verses from the psalms, some of which are Offertories from the Mass Proper: it is possible, then, that these had a specific place in the liturgy at Munich.

Few motets were published in the last nine years of Lassus's life, though Boetticher[8] suggests that the double-choir version of *Omnes de Saba* (posthumously issued) belongs to this period. This festive Epiphany piece is scored for equal choirs spanning a huge vocal range of well over three octaves. As in eight-part pieces generally, Lassus writes much for the tutti and less in dialogue, though the short overlapping phrases of 'Reges Tharsis' and the final 'Alleluia' provide exciting moments. His final, six-part volume of motets appeared at Graz five weeks before his death in 1594. The texts are partly concerned with death and deliverance, as befitted the spiritual morbidity that had overtaken the composer, but there is still room for mild humour in another eulogy of the joys of wine, *Luxuriosa res vinum*, whose words Lassus may well have written himself. On an altogether higher plane is the moving tribute to his own art in *Musica Dei donum*, a deeply felt setting of three Latin verses highlighting the word 'musica'. This is given a characteristic motive to unify the motet:

Ex. 15

The one category of works that has been omitted from the foregoing survey is the complete psalm setting. Lassus's motet corpus includes some thirty-four of these, spanning his career and ranging between three- and twelve-part scorings (though tending to favour larger textures and to be divided up into several *partes* on a grand scale). A number of features distinguish them from the type of setting coming into vogue in Italy after 1550. First, they were published in motet collections, not psalm collections specifically intended for use in a choral Office; secondly, they do not share with the latter the use of Gregorian psalm tones nor the *alternatim* scheme of performance whereby polyphony alternates with plainsong verses[9]; and thirdly, they do not include the doxology ('Gloria Patri') normally added at the

---

[8] Boetticher, op. cit., p. 562.
[9] The only exception is the six-part *In exitu Israel* (1581).

end of Office psalmody. For these reasons, many have regarded them as belonging to the 'psalm-motet' repertory begun by Josquin and inspired by a humanist spirit (personal choice of texts, freedom from traditional device) which also explains their importance to the early Lutheran composers of Protestant Germany. However, since no less than two-thirds of Lassus's psalms coincide with those required for Vespers and Compline (the two offices adorned with music at the Munich court chapel) on various major feasts, Sundays, and week-days, it is arguable that they might have been used in their correct position in the liturgy, as well as providing devotional music. The lack of a doxology need have posed no problem provided these words were recited by the clergy (in any case, many of Lassus's Mass settings similarly fail to set the final Agnus Dei ending 'dona nobis pacem'). Such a practice, though some might regard it as an abuse, could well have been tolerated at Munich.

In style, Lassus's psalms are not notably different from his motets. For instance, the double-choir *In convertendo* (Paris, 1565) bears out what has been said about his approach to polychoral writing, though with a lengthier text there is more time for each choir to be deployed separately. The two *partes* each set four verses of the psalm and proceed from longish passages for each of the two choirs, through more rapidly alternating dialogue and tutti effects, to a solid, extended eight-part conclusion. The four-part *Beatus vir* (Nuremberg, 1568) is one of the only two psalms to set the doxology: a verse-by-verse setting, it is written for male voices in a perhaps somewhat routine style until the vivid textual imagery of verse 9 jogs Lassus's musical imagination ('he shall gnash his teeth and melt away; the desire of the wicked shall perish'):

Ex. 16

This passage illustrates a sudden outbreak of rapid crotchet movement, in villanella fashion. Sometimes this kind of writing would dominate a whole psalm, as in the six-part *Cum invocarem* (Munich, 1570). The relentless declamation to short note-values hardly lets up until (significantly) the verse 'in pace . . . requiescam' ('I shall sleep in peace'), and persists through a turbulently rhythmic verse for just three voices. In the 1570s this villanella influence (sensationally termed 'the villanella crisis' by Boetticher) became even stronger: the six-part *Domine quid multiplicati* (Munich, 1582) proceeds entirely by rhythmically articulated block chords without a single suspension, nor scarcely any word repetition until the end. The bracketed metrical figure occurs frequently, and the whole psalm text of eight verses is dispatched in fifty-eight bars:

Ex. 17

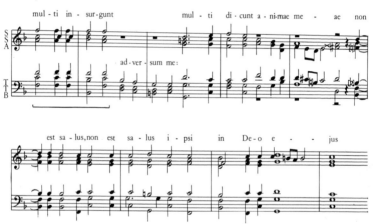

Lassus's Seven Penitential Psalms are a coherent group of works quite distinct from these others and represent perhaps the peak of his sacred output. They were composed about 1560 and, within a few years, copied into a huge parchment choirbook lavishly decorated with illustrations by the court painter Hans Mielich, which provide fascinating pictures of Lassus with his musicians. The psalms were not actually published until 1584, and were therefore 'reserved' for the private use of Lassus's patron: hence the definition of the term *musica reservata* by Lowinsky, who argues that its aim was to bring the emotion of the words vividly to life — 'rem quasi actam ante oculos ponere', in the words of the humanist writer Samuel Quickelberg, one of Lassus's admirers at the Munich court.[10] Boetticher sees *musica reservata* as a specifically German phenomenon, springing from aesthetic discussion.

Considering they were written in youth, these works sound unbelievably mature, with their sombre-hued sonorities and deeply spiritual atmosphere. Scarcely a trace of the conservative Netherlands tradition remains, and there is much that is forward-looking, especially in the matter of verbal declamation. Semi-liturgical connotations (e.g. repentance after confession, or devotional meditation after the Office of Matins and Lauds) fuse with intense personal feeling to produce music that is essentially private. Unlike Lassus's other psalms, these all have a separate musical section for every verse, and include the doxology: some of them are extremely long — Psalm 101 has thirty-one verses altogether, lasting forty minutes in performance; and one (Psalm 129) is even based on a Gregorian psalm tone, heard in each verse in various voices, and sometimes transposed or treated in canon. This relatively short *De profundis* is no less profound for its compositional device: in fact the reiterated chanting note A of the psalm tone enhances the music, causing many minor chords on D or A to darken the harmony despite the major mode, or beautifully offsetting the melismatic lower voices in verse 7, a *tricinium*:

Ex. 18

In all the psalms Lassus varies the scorings from time to time, and adds an extra voice by way of climax at the 'Sicut erat'.

Lastly, there remain the *Prophetiae Sibyllarum* (Sibylline Prophecies). Again, these could be viewed as *musica reservata*, for they

[10] Lowinsky, op. cit., p. 92.

17

were preserved in a manuscript of 1560 (adorned by a portrait of Lassus which proclaims his age to be twenty-eight) but only printed in 1600. In fact, the music almost certainly dates from his Italian years before 1555. It sets a cycle of humanistic Latin verse inspired by the Naples legend that the caves at nearby Cumae were the home of the Sibyls, who in ancient times foretold the coming of God. A series of twelve frescoes by Pinturicchio in the Borgia apartments at Rome suggested the ordering of the pieces to Lassus. He wrote them in a highly chromatic style made fashionable in Italy at the time through the efforts of modernists like Vicentino, but preserved a painstakingly clear declamation of the words and a lucid harmonic clarity. The prologue provides the *locus classicus* of this chromaticism, described by Lowinsky as 'triadic atonality', but perhaps a more representative extract would be the beginning of the seventh piece, *Sibylla Hellespontiaca*:

Ex. 19

Notice the chromatic alteration in the third bar, and the subtle change from F sharp to D major in bars 4–6. This is mysterious, brooding music, but never unsettling emotionally in the manner of Gesualdo. Lassus hardly ever used the style in any of his other works.

THE MASSES

IT used to be held that Lassus's Masses were inferior to his motets and certainly to the Masses of Palestrina, a view born largely out of ignorance, since the old collected edition included none of the Masses. It is only now that the new series is rectifying the situation, by bringing them all out and enabling balanced evaluations to be made. Chronology still presents problems since many of them survive only in manuscript, and the remainder were often printed well after composition. Moreover, there are a number of Masses whose attribution to Lassus is doubtful, or which survive in a fragmentary state, so that the reliable total of complete works is fifty-eight rather than the seventy of the collected edition. The following statistics are based on the former figure. There are nineteen *à 4*, twenty-one *à 5*, fifteen *à 6* and three *à 8*; no less than forty-eight are parody Masses, and eight are based on plainchant (leaving two unidentified); of the parody Masses, Lassus based seventeen on his own models, almost exclusively sacred motets, and thirty-one on models by other composers, almost exclusively secular pieces — an interesting contrast.

Only a handful of Masses belong to the Italian and Antwerp years up to 1556, and most of these are based on plainsong—the three Ferial Masses and the Missa Paschalis. Though Lassus must certainly have known Palestrina's early Masses, there is hardly a trace of the Roman's influence, but rather a harking back to the manner of older German composers like Senfl and Dietrich, who likewise wrote Masses upon plainsong. The one parody Mass of this youthful period is that based on Jacquet of Mantua's *Domine non secundum actum*, a typical five-part motet of the Gombert generation of Franco-Flemings.[1] Lassus's procedure in the Kyrie is to quote the first twenty bars of the model more or less exactly and add a further ten which expound one idea more fully, for Kyrie I; in the Christe, bars 31–42 follow bars 22–33 of the model, again with a few bars of continuation; for Kyrie II, Lassus starts with an original exposition of a much later point, and cleverly 'picks up' the final bars of the model to continue the section. There is

---

[1] All models by composers other than Lassus which the latter used for his parody Masses are printed in *Sämtliche Werke: Neue Reihe*, xii (Kassel, 1975).

no doubt that, right from the outset, his parody technique was not only admirable in itself but rich in fascinating insights for us today. In the early Masses, the Gloria would be divided into four *partes*, with fresh starts at 'Domine Deus' and 'Cum Sancto' as well as the usual 'Qui tollis', and pictorial writing would tend to occur at 'descendit de caelis' in the Credo.[2]

In his first ten years or so at Munich Lassus branched out in the writing of Masses, and especially in his choice of models, which ranged from the half-dozen lightweight chansons *à 4* of Sermisy, Certon, and others, through more serious chansons by Gombert and Crecquillon or a Willaert madrigal, to motets of his own in up to six parts. The four-part Masses based on more or less frivolous little chansons were partly responsible for earning Lassus's Masses a bad name in recent times. This is quite unjustified: they should be taken for what they are, simple functional music for lesser liturgical occasions, despite the secular connotations that might have brought a frown to Rome-based authorities in this era of musical purification.[3] In any case, short-winded models appealed to a composer with such a sense of the succinct. Lassus's Mass on Sermisy's chanson *Pilons pilons lorge*, for example, has a Kyrie just twenty-two bars long, though still in the usual three sections. Jogtrot chordal writing, which sets out from almost unaltered quotation of the model, dominates the Hosanna, where triple time speeds up bars 36–40 of the chanson and changes the accents, and the Gloria and Credo, though there are inventive moments at 'et homo factus est' where the final chords of the chanson are spun out by augmentation so as to slow the music down in a gesture of genuflection, as it were. Lupi's *Puisque j'ay perdu* was a model with a more elevated tone and a far greater independence of part writing despite its line-by-line approach to the text; this is reflected in the dignified style of Lassus's parody of it, which spreads the vocal range from two to nearly three octaves, and allows time to dwell at length on individual musical ideas. Here the triple-time Hosanna is a complete paragraph, developing a point first heard at bar 18 of the chanson in a manner reminiscent of one or two of Josquin's Hosannas (e.g. *Missa de beata Virgine, Pange lingua*). The Benedictus, reducing to three voices, begins with nine bars of flowing, melismatic counterpoint to an original point, but spends the remaining eighteen elaborating an idea

[2] M. Steinhardt, 'The *Missa Si me tenes*: a problem of authorship', *Aspects of Medieval and Renaissance Music*, ed. J. LaRue (London, 1966), pp. 760 ff.

[3] For example the Jesuits, who in Paris banned the performance of Lassus Masses at the Jesuit college there.

from bars 6–9 of the model (Ex. 20). Notice the two-bar pedal note, and the fact that Lassus delays his most exact 'version' of the model till bars 84–7, only to vary this with a different bass by way of conclusion:

Ex. 20

Not only is this an excellent illustration of his parody method, it also has all the technical fluency of Palestrina's Benedictus *tricinia*.

One of the very few secular models of his own was the chanson *Susanne un jour*, and to judge from the number of sources both printed and manuscript it seems that the Mass of that name enjoyed wide popularity. One of the prints was the sumptuous *Missae variis concentibus ornatae* brought out by the composer's Paris publishers Le Roy and Ballard in 1577/8 as part of a projected definitive edition of his Masses. Written in five parts like the model, this Mass contains a considerable quantity of original writing, departing quickly from the chanson though always setting out from a version of the opening at the start of each movement. By the Sanctus, all that remains of this is the rising idea (S, T1, T2), the falling triad (A, B) having been replaced by a fresh counterpoint; the Agnus, however, discards the rising idea, placing the falling triad in S, T1, and T2 against this same counterpoint in A and B.

Lassus wrote no six-part Masses until about 1565, but a number of distinguished works appeared thereafter. The *Missa Dixit Joseph* is a representative example from the late 1560s, based on his own motet of that name. Divided into two *partes*, the model emphasizes textural contrasts, often treating the three upper and lower parts like separated choirs. This is less evident in the Mass: although Kyrie I echoes the start of the motet with its SAA-TBB-tutti scoring, the next antiphonal passage ('pater noster senior') of the motet is not drawn upon till 'et in unum' of the Credo. The Christe and Kyrie II both contain passages of extra material linking quotations from the model: Kyrie II starts with the first seven bars of *pars II* of the motet, continues working the same points for four more bars, and concludes by jumping to the final fifteen bars of the motet. These same extracts are clearly audible at the Hosanna (triple time creating exciting cross-accents) and final 'miserere' of the Agnus Dei, respectively.[4] But perhaps these compositional subtleties are best illustrated by the gradual transformations of the very opening bars of the motet through each movement of the Mass:

Ex. 21

---

[4] Lassus normally set only one Agnus Dei verse, ending 'miserere nobis', and omitting the words 'dona nobis pacem' altogether.

The years around 1570 saw Lassus turning from French towards Italian models in the secular field, though his Mass on Sandrin's exquisite *Doulce memoire* dates from this time and is one of the most attractive Masses *à la française*. True, it has its proportion of plain block chordal writing in Gloria and Credo, but no contemporary listener would have missed the chanson's opening chords at 'resurrectionem mortuorum', to be followed by its closing bars at 'et vitam venturi saeculi. Amen'. This is the parody scheme of the Sanctus:

Lassus		Sandrin	
bar 1	Sanctus	Doulce memoire	bars 1–6
bar 9	Dominus Deus	O siècle	bars 9–13
bar 20	Dominus Deus	Or maintenant	bars 14–17
bar 25	Pleni sunt	(free)	
bar 37	Hosanna	le mal (bass only)	bars 28–32

To develop in imitation one line from the original is an imaginative stroke at the Hosanna. The 'Pleni sunt' has 'eye-music' for heaven and earth, and lends harmonic variety by modulating to F (the Dorian-mode chanson had no F cadences). But perhaps the most touching moment of all is the ending of the Agnus Dei, its unfolding sequence on 'miserere' leading to an anguished transformation of Sandrin's final cadence:

Lassus was always discriminating in the way he used the more striking passages of his model. For instance, in the Mass on Arcadelt's madrigal *Quand'io pens' al martire* (1569), he reserves until the Hosanna (always the joyous climax of his Masses) the use of the rapid crotchet movement of the madrigal (bars 30f.). Likewise the only moment of jerky rhythm that disturbs the serenity of Rore's five-part madrigal *Qual donna s'attende* ('con leggiadria', bars 32–3) is kept appropriately for the words 'gloriam tuam' in the Gloria of Lassus's fine Mass on this model. Modally, the Rore piece is quite bland: F Ionian with just a few B naturals or E flats. What Lassus does is to expand the harmonic scope with many further accidentals, especially at the end of the Credo, which sounds quite chromatic (bars 149–53). This 'colouring' is best seen in the gorgeous 'Qui tollis' of the Gloria, which takes as its starting point a simple chord progression that begins Rore's *seconda parte*:

Ex. 23

The 'Et incarnatus' of the Credo is similar. By contrast, the quite literal return to Rore's music at 'che quei dolci lumi' for the 'miserere nobis' at the very end of the Mass makes a touching conclusion.

This work probably dates from the later 1570s. So does the earlier of Lassus's two settings of the Requiem Mass, in four parts, written for an ATTB choir of narrow range with much crossing of parts and little use of a plainsong *cantus firmus*. On a much more exalted musical level stands the five-part Requiem (1580). Despite a sombre yet radiant spirituality that invites comparison with the Penitential Psalms, this setting is wedded to the liturgical ritual by its plainsong basis: a tenor part carries the *cantus firmus* in traditional fashion and the intonations are extraordinarily set in a very low bass register.

Lassus's three double-choir Masses date from the late 1570s and early 1580s. *Vinum bonum*, based on the secular motet of that name, is the earliest. *Bell' Amfitrit'altera*, whose madrigal model is so far unidentified but is possibly Venetian, suggests that in performance Lassus's choirs were not spaced far apart, for the textural contrasts are as likely to be between groups drawn from both choirs as between the two SATB choirs themselves (e.g. Hosanna: ATBB versus SSAT). His subtle ear for sonority could certainly be said to match that of his Venetian colleague Andrea Gabrieli. As for parody technique in double-choir music, that is best observed in the Mass upon his own motet *Osculetur me*, in which the two choirs are more self-contained. The Kyrie, though forty-six bars long, is spun out of just the first twenty-four bars of the motet, with a certain amount of transposed repetition, and the reworking of four-part music *à 8* and vice versa; the solid tutti chord progression (motet, bars 21–4) makes a fitting close.

In the longer movements, a more patchwork approach to the model is apparent, as in the first section of the Credo:

	Mass		motet
bar 1	Patrem omnipotentem	Osculetur	bars 1–7 modified
bar 9	visibilium	Quia meliora	bars 8–14 divided between choirs
bar 14	Et in unum	fragrantia	bar 14 altered
bar 18	Filium Dei	adolescentulae	bar 26 altered
bar 21	Et ex Patre	Trahe me	bar 30 altered to modulate
bar 24	ante omnia	in Cellaria	bar 43
bar 34	de Deo vero	super vinum	bar 54
bar 42	per quem omnia	Introduxit me	bar 40 altered to tutti
bar 47	Qui propter	adolescentulae	bar 26 altered, with free 'answer'
bar 51	descendit	effusum	bars 19–24

Since its model has a text from the Song of Songs, this Mass probably graced some feast of the Blessed Virgin or one of the female saints.

Of the few Masses dating from Lassus's old age, that on Gombert's chanson *Triste depart* (1592) is a fine example — an apt choice of model for the composer's valedictory frame of mind. The five-part chanson, written some fifty years earlier, is typical of its day in its continuously flowing imitative counterpoint and severe Dorian mode. Lassus, as expected, colours the harmony with accidentals, and varies the opening point at the beginning of each movement to achieve fresh contrapuntal possibilities. But for the 1590s this is decidedly not progressive music: Lassus's reworkings of his models tell us less about the development of style over the years that separate parody and original than, say, Palestrina's reworkings of his predecessors' music, and it is not in the Masses that we should seek Lassus's 'late style'. Where they do instruct is in matters of compositional procedure. Take the bold rising scales of 'ma face avoit perdu', the final point (bar 36) of the Gombert chanson (Ex. 24a) which provides the conclusion for each movement of the Mass except the Sanctus:

Ex. 24

(a)

(Gombert)

Ma face a-voit per-du tout-te   cou-leur

In the Kyrie Lassus alters the part writing to increase the vocal span; in the Gloria he quotes it more literally, expanding it on repetition, an ideal musical garb for 'in gloria Dei Patris'; the rhythms are much more taut in the Credo (naturally arising out of a twenty-bar passage of nervously agitated writing since 'et unam'); whereas in the Agnus Dei scarcely more than the harmonic substance remains:

(b)

(Lassus)

Ky - ri - - - - e

(c)

et vi - tam

et vi - tam ven - tu - ri sae - - - - cu - li et vi - tam

et vi - tam

et vi - tam

Ex. 24

(d)

If this all too brief survey of the Masses has been weighted towards parodies of secular models, it is to show Lassus's powers as one who could ennoble modest music in such a way as to provide a fitting adornment to the liturgy, even if in a manner contrary to the strict intention of the Tridentine reforms.

OTHER LITURGICAL WORKS

UNDER this heading belong the works Lassus wrote for specific use in the liturgy: the hymns and Canticle settings for Vespers and Compline (the two Offices sung chorally at Munich), the Passions, Lamentations, and Responsories for Holy Week, and certain music for particular feastdays such as Christmas.

Lassus set two cycles of Lessons from the Book of Job, which are read at Matins in the Office of the Dead; the first was an early work, written in his first years at Munich, and, like the Penitential Psalms, reserved for the Duke's private use until its publication in 1565. Once again, gloomy texts seem to have inspired him to some of the finest four-part music he ever wrote. The third section of Lesson VIII (*Pelli meae*) has become well known as a motet in its own right, *Scio enim* ('I know that my Redeemer liveth'), words which shine like a ray of hope amid the murk of stark pessimism. This is Lassus in his most persuasively fervent rhetorical vein, using a wide chromatic vocabulary (all twelve semitones) though reserving the remote D sharp for the startling 'et non alius' ('whom my eyes shall behold, and not another'):

Ex. 25

Texts like these allowed Lassus's musical imagination free rein, as in the motets. In the miscellaneous liturgical works issued under the title of *Officia* in Part III of the *Patrocinium musices* in 1574, on the other hand, the traditional *cantus firmus* method, of anchoring the music securely to the ritual plainsong, is in evidence. Part IV of the *Patrocinium* (1575) included the earliest of his four Passions, the St. Matthew, which retains the usual plainsong for the parts of the Evangelist and Christus, but sets those of other single characters in two- or three-part polyphony, and the *turba* part of course for full choir in five parts.[1] The same scheme is found in the St. John Passion, but the St. Mark and St. Luke have polyphony only for the four-part *turba* choruses, since they were sung on lesser days in Holy Week.

Like Victoria, Lassus found great inspiration in the Lamentations and Responsories for the Office of Tenebrae in Holy Week, of which he wrote settings in the early 1580s. Both composers wrote a cycle of three Lamentations for each of the last three days of that week, leaving the intervening Responsories to be sung in plainsong; in the two later portions of the service (Nocturns), however, they set the Responsories to polyphony, leaving the intervening lessons to be chanted, a scheme which preserved the ritual alternation of plainsong and polyphony throughout the long Office. Lassus's Lamentations, in five parts, are most impressive works, and have suffered shameful neglect; they stand in complete contrast to the detached impersonality of Palestrina's. The Maundy Thursday set are written in the sombre A-Phrygian mode, often darkened still further by E flats, as at the opening:

Ex. 26

---

[1] An extra, sixth voice is added in the 'Crucifigatur' and 'Vere Filius Dei' choruses.

The Hebrew letters prefacing each verse are set in the usual flowing melismatic manner (Ex. 27), and particularly poignant harmonies occur at the cry 'Jerusalem' at the end of the second Lamentation (Ex. 28), with affecting semitones and drooping intervals:

Ex. 27

Ex. 28

In the first, the mere word 'requiem' prompts a momentary quotation of plainsong from the Requiem Mass, a typical instance of Lassus's fondness for symbolic musical punning. The Tenebrae Responsories survive only in manuscript, and are more modestly written for four voices. Compared with the well-known Victoria settings, they are terser, more homophonic, and more dramatic; in the *versus* Lassus reduces to two voices. Major modes (as in the set for Maundy Thursday second Nocturn) are often coloured by minor inflections that add harmonic tension.

The settings of the Magnificat for Vespers and the Nunc dimittis for Compline represent a significant yet again totally neglected part of Lassus's sacred output (this neglect is because the sources are mainly in manuscript and still await a systematic edition).[2] He wrote no less than 101 Magnificats, most of them in later life, when he was well established at Munich. Like the Masses, many of these are parody pieces based on existing musical models, which include not only sacred motets but also — uniquely to Lassus — works in quite different

² The author is grateful to Clive Wearing for making his transcriptions of some of these works available for study.

genres, particularly madrigals and villanellas, a radically new departure in Continental Magnificat settings. The early 1580s was the most productive period for those based on Italian models, which included older pieces by men such as Arcadelt, Verdelot, Rore, and Berchem, and astonishingly recent ones too (e.g. G. M. Nanino's *Erano i capei d'oro*, which Lassus would have found alongside some of his own madrigals in Phalèse's famous anthology *Musica divina* of 1583).[3] Perhaps one of the most dignified and impressive parody Magnificats is that upon Josquin's *Praeter rerum seriem* in six parts (1582). The model was of venerable antiquity: Lassus, setting the even-numbered verses as usual (the odd-numbered being sung to a plainsong psalm tone of appropriate mode), sets out from close adherence to the model towards a richly varied treatment, reflecting the way in which Josquin himself gradually moves away from the solemn *cantus firmus* presentation of the original plainsong in his motet. At the opposite extreme stand settings like the Magnificat *primi toni à 4* published in 1567, which has hardly a shred of contrapuntal elaboration and often falls into the jogtrot crotchet declamation of his Glorias and Credos:

Ex. 29

Apart from a few vestigial references to the plainsong psalm tone, this is freely composed, but many of the non-parody Magnificats are based on a strict presentation of the psalm tone in the tenor, even if the style is quite chordal.

A dozen settings of the shorter Canticle Nunc dimittis survive, again a mixture of *cantus firmus* and parody treatments. Paradoxically the shorter text invites a more measured approach than in the short-winded Magnificats, and the four-part pieces of *c.*1570 present a

---

[3] Boetticher, 'Anticipations of Dramatic Monody in the Late Works of Lassus', *Essays on Opera and English Music*, ed. F. W. Sternfeld and others (Oxford, 1975), p. 90.

resourceful blend of syllabic writing and flowing melisma, the psalm tone permeating other voices than the tenor which carries it. Verse 4 ('Lumen ad revelationem') is sometimes given a reduced texture: a two-part canon in the *quarti toni* five-part setting, and a symbolic *tricinium* for the three high parts in the parody setting *Heu mihi Domine*. It is fascinating that this latter piece, written as late as 1592, should be based on the composer's own early Antwerp motet of nearly forty years before.

THE MADRIGALS AND VILLANELLAS

LASSUS first proclaimed himself to the world as a madrigalist at the age of twenty-three. The year 1555 saw the publication in Antwerp of a multi-lingual compilation of four-part pieces dominated by Italian settings and in Venice of his first book of five-part madrigals. We shall leave the villanellas until the end of this chapter; the six in the Antwerp print were matched by six madrigals, which were the earliest of the 175 or so that Lassus composed. It is worth noting that the print itself was among the first volumes of madrigals ever to appear outside Italy, and proved so popular that Susato had to reissue it again in the same year. (Further evidence of popularity was that at least one of the madrigals — to say nothing of the catchy villanellas — circulated widely in instrumental arrangements.)[1]

In a way, there is nothing surprising about Lassus's enthusiastic espousal of the madrigal genre, for he spent his most formative years in

---

[1] H. M. Brown, *Instrumental Music printed before 1600* (Cambridge, Mass., 1965); this madrigal (*Per pianto la mia carne*) was reprinted several times in its original form, as listed in R. A. Harman, *Popular Italian Madrigals of the Sixteenth Century* (London, 1976).

Italy, and it was during his period in Rome (1552-4) that he was best able to study the madrigal repertories both of that city and of Venice — the works of Arcadelt, Willaert, and Rore in particular. The activities of Antonio Barré, an alto in the choir at St. Peter's, and a noted collector and publisher of madrigals, would have been very helpful to him. From the very outset, the texts Lassus set tended towards the melancholy: Petrarch's *Occhi piangete*, with the drooping opening of its top line (a part full of delicate melodic curves) and exquisite sequential phrase 'lamentar più' at the end; or Ariosto's text *Queste non son più lagrime*, conceived in the quasi-chordal vein of the Roman *madrigale arioso*, an appellation which again stresses the tunefulness of Lassus's top part, a hallmark of these early four-part madrigals. The balanced shaping of each individual phrase can be seen in Ex. 30 within whose short span the rising idea 'non suppliron', delicately placed across the beat, is offset by a descent through a series of dissonances. As we can see from the internal stress scheme shown by brackets, even the top voice alone builds to a climax, to which the typical false relation in the harmony adds a final touch:

Ex. 30

Though the first book of five-part madrigals appeared at Venice, the second and third were issued in Rome by Barré in 1557 and 1563 respectively; much of the music in all three may well date from Lassus's Roman years. He was especially attracted to Petrarch at this time, and in the 1555 volume set texts such as *Cantai, or piango*, *Crudele acerba*, and *Solo e pensoso* that were well known in madrigal literature. While a comparison of his setting of the second of these with Rore's of about the same time reveals the latter to have been much more daring (anticipating in some ways the Wert setting of the late 1580s), there is striking evidence that Wert himself did know Lassus's *Solo e pensoso*. The disconsolate wandering of the poet is reflected in the modally vague, meandering melodic lines of Lassus, which take on their most exaggerated form in the bass: Wert seizes upon the super-imposed fifths of this voice's 'deserti campi' (bars 5-6) in fashioning his own opening point, or, put in another way, he extends the second interval of Lassus's opening idea to a fifth, giving it the over-all span of a ninth, something hardly conceivable as early as 1555 and before such 'mannerist' excesses were fashionable:[2]

Ex. 31

Lassus's piece as a whole continues to convey the searching qualities of the poem by destroying any feeling of modal orientation with a wide variety of unexpected accidentals; from the basic Ionian F major it reaches as far on the sharp side as E minor and B minor at the word 'aspre' ('bitter') (bar 52). But by bar 60 F has been regained, with suddenly static harmonies at 'ragionando' which again may have provided a cue for Wert's setting, where the whole of the final phrase of the poem is set to an extraordinarily inconclusive repeated chord.

[2] The Wert setting is printed in *Opera omnia*, ed. C. MacClintock (Corpus Mensurabilis Musicae 24), vii, 32; and in *Das Chorwerk*, lxxx, 1. See also C. MacClintock, *Giaches de Wert* (Rome, 1966), pp. 107–8. The word 'mannerist' applies here to the last decades of the sixteenth century: J. Roche, *The Madrigal* (London, 1972), pp. 73 ff., expresses the author's view on 'mannerism', but further divergent interpretations of the term are discussed by various scholars in *Studi musicali*, iv (1974).

Even in his early years, Lassus's taste ran to the genuinely spiritual as well as the merely reflective type of text: the words of *Quanto il mio duol* (from the first book of four-part madrigals of 1560) are indeed of this kind, addressed to the Deity rather than the ubiquitous beloved, and in this they prefigure his much later madrigals. The music is sober enough, with mildly dissonant passing notes for 'with voice of sorrow' and the sudden quickening to *note nere* (black notes, i.e. crotchets) for 'come then, my madness'. In vain would we seek any extremes of expression in this or any other of Lassus's early madrigals: the chromatic semitone, for instance, is rarely found, let alone the modish chromaticism of the *Prophetiae Sibyllarum*; they unite an Italian spirit with the most recent Netherlandish tradition, and inhabit the world of Willaert and Rore.

This world Lassus had decidedly left by the time he published his fourth book of five-part madrigals in 1567. It was the fruit of his first years at Munich, the proof that his madrigalian interests could continue to flourish even on German soil. In this particular year he was in Venice, and could oversee the publication in person; he then travelled to Ferrara to present the volume to Duke Alfonso II d'Este, but its reception was unfortunately cool. This seems odd if we examine the music, which includes two imposing cycles of madrigals in six sections each, and a setting of Petrarch's moving *I'vo piangendo* that exudes stylistic confidence in its use of musical subtleties in the service of the words. In the first part of this madrigal, Lassus demonstrates his complete command of rhythmic 'pacing' by means of alternations of minim and crotchet movement; in the second, he plunges straight in with the latter, as the words 'war and tempest' suggest, and then dramatically holds back for 'I may die in peace and in safe harbour', colouring the harmony with a magical false relation:

Ex. 32

Four-part pieces in this mature, perhaps 'middle period', style include two from another of Lassus's multi-lingual collections, published in Munich in 1573: *Sotto quel sta* and *Spesso in poveri alberghi*, to two strongly contrasted texts from Ariosto's *Orlando furioso*. The first of these moves along placidly until the top part takes wing in a delightful melisma where the words speak of the beloved's smiles causing earth to seem like paradise. The second, on the other hand, has words which attack the unfriendly atmosphere found in courtly palaces: interpreted by some as a protest against earthly power and social injustice, it may be no coincidence that it was written shortly before Lassus's relations with Duke Albrecht, his patron, deteriorated.[3] On the musical plane, it illustrates well what Einstein termed the 'conciseness and impatience' of his madrigal style. Into a bare twenty-five bars Lassus packs tension in the form of uneasy harmonic changes, distant modulations in a flatward direction (even just before the end, which sounds unsettled and inconclusive), and jarring syncopations; there is hardly a melisma in sight, and the madrigal is impelled by a relentless crotchet movement.

Lassus's madrigal output was in fact rather sporadic in these middle years, and no publication exclusively devoted to them was issued between 1567 and 1585. Apart from the Munich print just mentioned, we have to turn to a chanson collection, the *Mellange* of 1576, to find a further handful of five-part madrigals included as an appendage. These would seem to date from the mid-1570s, and again illustrate classical contrasts of mood from one to another. In *Ove le luci giro* and *Che più d'un giorno* the music is bursting with rhythmic energy, and the crotchet movement is more pervasive than the conventional minims of the *misura di breve*. The spirited ending of the latter madrigal (Ex. 33) shows Lassus twice painting the final word 'dies' with a false relation (see also Ex. 32 above):

Ex. 33

(The selfsame false relation paints the same image at the end of Gesualdo's *Luci serene e chiare*, where it of course sounds compara-

[3] Boetticher, op. cit., p. 406.

tively mild; but for Lassus it was about as far as one could go in the realms of harmonic juxtaposition in a madrigal, and is all the more effective in a piece that has scarcely any dissonance at all.) In *Madonna sa l'amor*, however, the music moves largely in minims, and the mode is sombre and Phrygian. Here we find one of Lassus's characteristic punning 'signatures' of his name in its Italian form (Lasso = la sol in solmization syllables, i.e. the notes A and G, or D and C): this is clearly audible at the start of the piece's most dissonant passage (Ex. 34). The 'interrupted' V-IV cadence is entirely typical of his predilection for harmonic side-stepping:

Ex. 34

By the 1580s we have reached Lassus's last phase as a madrigalist. An important source for the early years of the decade is another collection issued in Paris and given over mainly to chansons, *Continuation du mellange* of 1584, the madrigals of which now show a distinct preference for fewer dissonances, syllabic writing within each vocal part, and, sometimes, for absolutely chordal textures. This is especially true of his setting of Petrarch's *Dapoi che sotto'l ciel*, where the interest is primarily rhythmic, as when all five voices enunciate the opening words in the purest speech rhythm:

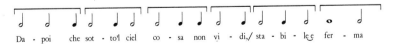

Such declamation also appears in the fine setting of Ariosto's words *Deh perchè voglio*. Lack of space prevents the examination of its many felicitous details. Suffice it to quote this short passage from near the end of the *seconda parte*, where Lassus prepares the music for a striking 'descent from heaven' by repeating the first phrase with intensifying crotchet movement in the lower parts:

Ex. 35

Among the 1584 pieces are two homage madrigals whose words also may be by Lassus. They are in praise of Duke Wilhelm and may well have been performed at the ceremonies which inaugurated his rule when he succeeded his father Albrecht in 1579. Then there are the attractive 'night pieces' *Come la notte* and *Come lume di notte*, the latter delicately scored for four high voices. Lastly, a dialogue for two five-part choirs, *Passan vostri trionfi*, apes the current Venetian manner, and was indeed reissued at Venice in 1590.

The picture of the late madrigal is filled out by two Nuremberg collections of 1585 and 1587, whose titles proclaim them as newly composed. Taken as a whole, these works show that Petrarch remained Lassus's favourite poet, and that when not setting his words the composer's taste inclined to those of religious Petrarchists like Fiamma, whose cycle of six poems beginning *Per aspro mar* received a noble setting in the 1587 volume. Not for Lassus the frivolities of fashionable pastoral verse by such men as Guarini. The spiritual or ethical atmosphere predominates; the poetry is of resignation, reflecting upon the transitoriness of life. Such a renunciation of the conventional love lyric owes much to the over-fervid Counter-Reformation zeal of Duke Wilhelm's court, which brought an atmosphere of introspection and joylessness of life that seems to have adversely affected Lassus's health. But the music represents the absolute peak of his madrigal output. It ranges from restrained four-part pieces like *Deh, lascia, anima* and the sestina *Per aspro mar*, in which the opening, with its insecure sense of harmonic direction (Ex. 36), well portrays the troubled, questing soul:

Ex. 36

Per a - spro mar di not - te in picciol le - gno

to the most impressive six-part settings of sonnets by Fiamma: *Il grave de l'età* and *Ben sono i premi*, characterized by their dense counter-point, dramatic pauses, virtuoso vocal writing, and brilliant contrasts of texture. It may well be that, compared with the immensely popular Marenzio and the radical, mannerist Wert, whose names tend to dominate the madrigal history of the 1580s, Lassus was no more a modernist in matters of musical style than in his taste in poetry, but that is not to say that he was altogether impervious to newer trends. The style of vocal writing and the textural contrasts are indeed up to date: there is more than a hint of Marenzio in the scurrying quavers of the ending to *Il grave de l'età*:

Ex. 37

i tuoi di - let - ti, i tuoi, i tuoi di - let - ti.

In the five-part *Hor vi riconfortate* of 1585 we find examples of other 'modernisms' often credited to Marenzio: the bright SSATB scoring, in which the two upper parts seem to stand apart in pseudo-concertato fashion (especially, as here, when supported just by the alto for short snatches), and the syllabic quaver declamation later to become so typical of the early Baroque. It has also been said that there are pre-Baroque qualities in Lassus's swan-song and farewell to the madrigal, the remarkable *Lagrime di S. Pietro* which appeared just three weeks before his death in 1594. These qualities reside not in the musical details but in the spiritual fervour of this setting of twenty-one poems by Tansillo which Lassus dedicated to Pope Clement VIII. He wrote it in austere seven-part counterpoint, as what Haar aptly describes as 'a magnificent tonal arch covering the whole range of sixteenth-century sound'.[4] It was at once his artistic testament to posterity and the culmination of both his musical maturity and his obsession with matters of the soul.

If the madrigals mostly represent Lassus in serious moods, the popular villanellas remind us that he was also a man of mordant wit, entirely conversant with the baser forms of musical expression. His presence in Naples in early youth accounts for the half-dozen villanellas included in the multi-lingual publication of 1555, for that city was the source of the *canzon villanesca* (to give the genre its full name). The music takes its cue from similar pieces by the Neapolitan pioneer of the genre, Gian Domenico da Nola, and also by Willaert, who helped to popularize it in northern Italy: a four-part texture, plenty of bright, major chords, and bouncing rhythms — the ideal vehicle for texts concerned with humbler aspects of the human condition. Many of these texts Lassus took from Nola; in addition, the music of four pieces is an elaboration of existing three-part villanellas by the Neapolitan Vincenzo Fontana, a technique which Willaert had already applied to Nola's works. Two of the 1555 villanellas, *La cortesia* and *Madonna mia pietà*, became especially popular in arrangements for instruments.[5] Much later in life, Lassus issued a whole volume of light pieces, *Villanelle, moresche, e altre canzoni*, at Paris in 1581. Some of these may have been hitherto unpublished early works from his time in Naples, but that he claimed to have written them 'in old age, when he should have known better' suggests that he was still turning his hand to the genre in Germany, perhaps to provide lusty songs for light entertainments at the court. Certainly the hilarious double-choir echo piece *O la, o che bon eccho* demands 'stage' and 'off-stage' groups for its performance, while the equally well-known *Matona mia cara* (properly a *tedesca* since it burlesques a German soldier attempting to serenade his lady-love in broken Italian) seems clearly inspired by Imperial military forays into Italy. The *moresche*, which gave Lassus a chance to turn his wit to Negro slaves, include the delightful *Hai Lucia*, with its bright, triadic call-to-attention and frequent progressions of major chords a second apart:

[4] Haar, op. cit.
[5] Brown, op. cit., lists six and seven arrangements respectively.

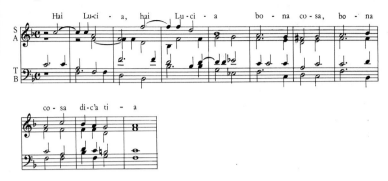

Block chords and simple dance-like rhythms are the stuff of this style, with hardly a trace of 'learned' imitation to be found, and the musical structure is basic and repetitive — shapes like *A–A–B–C–C* are particularly common, as in the charming love song *O occhi manza mia*. The text of this piece is innocuous enough; not so many of the others, which are as indelicate as those of some chansons, however smart their musical clothing.

By the 1580s the villanella was giving way to the canzonetta, an altogether more polished type of strophic setting. Though Lassus acknowledged this development in his *La non vol esser più mia* (1584), a bright five-part chordal piece which stands strikingly apart from the madrigals which surround it, and whose rigid dance-like metre looks forward to such works as Gastoldi's *balletti*, this was an isolated work, and Lassus seemed to be drawn naturally to the earthy raciness of the old villanella as an outlet for his sense of humour.

THE CHANSONS

L ASSUS's European fame in his own time rested to a considerable degree upon his output of French chansons. He wrote nearly 150 of them, all highly characteristic in their variety of moods and styles, and many among the best of the century. He was Arcadelt's natural successor as a writer of such pieces, and one can indeed follow the fortunes of the genre from the 1550s onwards for three decades through his contributions alone, though it is true that these became more sporadic in his later life. French was, of course, Lassus's mother tongue, and he would still have heard it spoken at the Munich court, where he wrote most of his finest chansons. He published chansons mainly in the Low Countries and Paris, where the printing firm of Le Roy and Ballard soon accorded him the appellation of 'divin Orlande'.

The first Lassus chansons to appear were the half-dozen for four voices in the multi-lingual Antwerp volume of 1555, which show that he was fully aware of the stylistic possibilities of the day. The first of them, *Las voulez-vous*, illustrates the fairly serious tone of some Netherlandish chanson writers like Gombert and Crecquillon, being mainly contrapuntal with restrained melismas on words like 'chanter'; even at this early date, the typical opening *exordium*, voices following close upon one another with sharply-etched motives, is in evidence. *Je l'ayme bien*, which begins with a more conventional imitation, has a delicate contrast in the 'pattering' crotchets of the middle section; the opening words and music return to round off the piece, an *A–B–A* scheme quite common in chansons. Perhaps the most catchy of these early pieces is *Vray Dieu disoit une fillette*, with its bright major key and fast syllabic word setting. The gaiety of this piece made it very popular with arrangers for lute and keyboard.[1] In a very different vein is *En espoir vis*, whose detailed word painting sticks out in an almost madrigalian way: at 'crainte me tourmente' a pedal note in the bass interrupts the harmonic flow as early as the sixth bar of the piece, while 'mais mon grief mal me contraint soupirer' inspires a 'gasping' effect no previous chanson composer could have contemplated (Ex. 39). Notice too the harmonic progression, a rapid circle of fifths from A to F that actually helps to create the tension:

[1] Brown, op. cit., gives nine arrangements.

The fruits of Lassus's early years at Munich in the chanson field were also published at Antwerp: the important first book of four-part chansons of 1564. In this Lassus paid special attention to that most celebrated poet of the chanson repertory, Clément Marot (there are no less than seven settings of his verses here). His poem *Qui dort icy?* is given a delightfully deft and intimate musical clothing: slow and long-drawn-out harmonies for Venus sleeping, a flurry of crotchets for 'if you wake her'. Other Marot settings include *Monsieur l'Abbé*, which pokes fun at a French clergyman and his valet who were over-inclined to drink the night away, and (on an even more indelicate note) *Fleur de quinze ans*, which Haar describes as 'a seduction piece of persuasive musical diction',[2] though making the point that on the whole chansons are not grand enough for the musico-rhetorical treatment of the motets. Particularly felicitous here is Lassus's use of triple time to broaden the first part of this 'lesson in love':

Ex. 40

Pierre de Ronsard was another poet favoured by Lassus. The setting of Ronsard's *Bon Jour mon coeur* was nothing less than a 'hit' of the time, with countless arrangements as sure evidence of its popularity. And no wonder: here the Italian sensuousness of harmony, especially pure major triads for their own sake (where a traditional Frenchman would have minor ones), comes out. For all its homophonic brevity, the piece is highly colourful, with frequent accidentals. Other popular pieces have this simple, direct manner: the bucolic harvest song *Margot*

[2] Haar, op. cit.

labourez les vignes, where the Italian villanella influence is even more obvious, and the ironic *Quand mon mari*, a wry comment on wife-beating in the peasant community, with its appealing narrative idiom, incisive rhythms, and pair alternations. Taking the chansons of Lassus's early Munich years as a whole, then, we find a mixture of love songs, laments, nature and harvest songs, reflections on lost happiness, fun at the expense of clerics, and indeed generally a plethora of *risqué* narratives. Lassus had a Rabelaisian streak when it came to satire or even blasphemy, and was quick to respond to accounts of human foibles, however bawdy. He could be utterly respectable, too, as in the innocent nature scene of *Soyons joyeux*, in which he cleverly varies the *A–B–A* scheme by coming back with an inversion of his opening triadic idea.

Lassus's five-part chansons seem neglected beside his four-part ones, though they are scarcely less important or less numerous, for in general he preferred the richer texture. Indeed, the most popular by far of his earlier chansons (judging again from arrangements but also from circulation in print and manuscript) was the five-part *Susanne un jour*, first published in 1560. Here we have a different type of chanson, to religious words recounting the Biblical tale of Susanna: Lassus based the music on the tenor of a minor French composer's setting of twelve years before, but disguised this to create a seamless musical flow and emphasize the top part of a bright, Italianate SSATB scoring. The piece is soberly polyphonic, with only a brief chordal passage. One of the many reprints was of an English-text version in *Musica transalpina* of 1588, though it had already appeared in London in 1570 along with a number of Protestant sacred 'parodies' of his chansons. In fact Lassus was probably the most published continental composer in the London of Queen Elizabeth I, and this particular Protestant adaptation of a Catholic's works (very necessary, for the earthiness of the original texts would have caused Protestant zealots to shake their heads) was at once a milestone and a token of Lassus's universality.[3] Not only prints, but also manuscripts testified to his fame in England. There are no less than ten sources of *Susanne*, and there is a song called *Mouncier Mingo* for use in Shakespeare's *Henry IV Part II*.

The original of this latter was *Un Jour vis un foulon*, a jaunty chordal piece that describes the pressing of wine. It appeared in the *Mellange* of Lassus chansons brought out by Le Roy and Ballard at Paris in 1570, a collection which by and large builds on the repertory of the

---

[3] F. W. Sternfeld, 'Vautrollier's printing of Lasso's *Recueil du mellange* (London: 1570)', *Annales musicologiques*, v (1957), pp. 199, 201–2.

1560s. Included in it are bawdy pieces like *En un Chasteau*, or mildly blasphemous ones such as *Je suis quasi prest d'enrager*, whose words contain the clever pun 'O benedicite Maria . . . le diable bien me maria', dependent of course on the fact that they are macaronic.

In 1571 Lassus paid his first visit to Paris, the centre where his published work was most appreciated, to dedicate a new book of five-part chansons to the French King, Charles IX. For his efforts he was awarded a special right to publish music in the city; one of the chansons in the book, *O Foible Esprit*, is a fine example of the stylistic dignity and slightly madrigalian intensity of its contents. It is set to a sonnet in the Petrarchan mould by Joachim du Bellay, in two *partes*: in the second Lassus 'speeds up' the motion to crotchets, much as he would in a madrigal, but at times the musical language reveals a Netherlandish origin (Ex. 41) in its restrained rising sixths and smooth, richly overlapping sequences:

Ex. 41

Here the texture is continuous. It is quite a different matter in *Si du malheur*, published in 1573 in another of Lassus's multi-lingual collections, where declamatory rests intervene and there is much rhythmic tension:

Ex. 42

Perhaps the culmination of this more madrigalian approach to the chanson comes in the well-known *La Nuict froide et sombre*. The words, by du Bellay, evoke the transformation from night to day; Lassus responds with an exquisite four-part setting which, as we would expect, reflects this by a gradual, superbly controlled progress from dark, long-held chords to brightly animated crotchet movement. Despite its mere thirty-five bars the piece abounds in felicitous details of scoring and colour: those who have called it a 'tone poem' scarcely exaggerate. It was first issued in 1576, in a revised and updated reprint of the *Mellange* of 1570.

Lassus tended to prefer other forms of secular music in his later life. The only further major publication of chansons was the *Continuation du mellange* of 1584. This provides some evidence that he was aware of the current fashion of *musique mesurée* (in fact his 1576 book had contained the first printed example of this style, *Une puce*) which favoured a strictly chordal declamation to long and short note values in classical metre. The following extract from the little three-part *Mais qui pourroit* illustrates this. As far as 'cacher' it might easily be a verset from one of Le Jeune's *chanson mesurés*, the purest manifestations of the genre; but the last bars (which open the refrain of this strophic chanson) recall something else again, the Italian villanella, so often written for just three voices:

Ex. 43

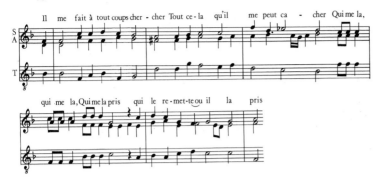

So here we have in fact a French *villanella*. This is not, however, representative of Lassus's late chansons, which suggest only a passing flirtation with the theories of *musique mesurée* as propounded by Baïf's *Académie*, even if they favour simplicity of style and comprehensibility of the words. A better example is the sober, lightly contrapuntal *Heureux qui met*, one of two chansons recently reconstructed through the rediscovery of a missing part in an English manuscript source. Here Lassus, characteristically for his later years, sets an ethical, moralizing text by de Pibrac, a French diplomat as well as poet. We may conclude this brief glance at Lassus's chansons by quoting the closing bars of the piece. Notice the odd passing note (marked with an asterisk) in the alto, which is irregularly 'resolved' in the tenor, and the rich part-writing of the penultimate, Phrygian cadence:

Ex. 44

THE LIEDER

L ASSUS took naturally to the composition of chansons, for French was his native language, and of madrigals, for Italian was the tongue of his musical education; but German was for him an adopted language, in which he was never to be entirely happy expressing himself. There are fewer lieder than chansons or madrigals — about ninety in all — and he settled less readily into writing them, for the first printed collection did not appear until 1567. None the less, this inaugurated a series of seven volumes stretching on until 1590 which profoundly affected the development of song in Germany.

Munich had for some time been an important centre of the German tenor-lied, which reached its zenith with the works of Ludwig Senfl (who died there in the early 1540s), and was widely popularized by Georg Forster's voluminous song anthologies. The *cantus firmus* style implicit in the label 'tenor-lied' also proved ideal for the early Lutheran composers who used chorale melodies as a basis for their settings. Indeed these melodies were often *contrafacta* of traditional secular tunes. Lassus soon became familiar with this tradition and the resemblance within it of sacred and secular idioms. Though a Catholic, he frequently set German sacred texts, which account for more than half of those he used. But in musical style he broke with tradition right from the start. There is no rigorous *cantus firmus* treatment in the setting of Luther's *Vater unser* melody which heads the 1567 publication. His debt to Senfl and Forster here lies more in the choice of texts well established in German taste than in the music, for he ignored the pronounced caesuras of their songs and introduced madrigalian touches. He could hardly have repressed the influence of his Italian experience, and it was his ability to express the words which was singled out by German theorists of later centuries.[1] A novelty to which he himself drew attention in the 1567 preface was the five-part texture, though this had been by no means uncommon in earlier lieder: it was more the way he used it (that is to create a sonorous tonal palette for its own sake rather than as a medium for the contrapuntal *tours-de-force* of a Senfl) that was new at the end of the century. *Ein guter Wein*

[1] R. Hinton Thomas, *Poetry and Song in the German Baroque* (Oxford, 1963), pp. 2 ff.

48

is a good example of these early lieder, with a typical text in praise of drink (in Lassus's case, wine rather than beer). Musical interest resides not in melody but in rhythmic word declamation and vocal scoring, and the song begins with the usual imitative *exordium* or call-to-attention:

Ex. 45

Lassus's second songbook, which came out in 1572, showed a greater respect for the age-old *cantus firmus* treatment, especially in the settings of sacred texts by Lutheran poets. Sometimes, however, a churchly style would be used in an ironic way, as in the narrative *Es jagt ein Jäger*: the first half of the piece presents the story of a huntsman as a quasi-dialogue between the upper and the lower voices in flowing counterpoint, hilariously interrupted by the blowing ('blasen') of his horn:

Ex. 46

A rather similar thing occurs at the start of *Audite nova! Der Bau'r von Eselskirchen*, where the Latin words are given ten bars of motet-like polyphony by way of introduction to a raucous ditty about a goose: it was the custom to roast this bird on the feast of St. Martin, and to add the finishing touches to the banquet with 'goose' songs like this. Such a macaronic piece comes appropriately from the multi-lingual collection of 1573 dedicated to the Fugger family and often called the *Viersprachendrück* on account of its mixture of Latin, French, Italian, and German settings, excellent proof of Lassus's cosmopolitanism. In 1576 came Lassus's third songbook proper, in which he felt it necessary to apologize for the 'German uncouthness' of the music, maybe because of his growing reputation as a madrigalist. A particularly sharp contrast between the lied and other secular genres can be drawn with the aid of *Susannen frumb* and the famous chanson *Susanne un jour* mentioned in the previous chapter. In the German setting Lassus preserves a more literal *cantus firmus* treatment of his borrowed tenor, without disguising its phrasing or directing emphasis to the top part. In other words, he chooses the musical procedures appropriate to the individual cultural milieu.[2]

The first three songbooks were all for five voices;[3] in 1583 a four-part collection appeared, at the head of which was a setting of the well-known old chorale *Christ ist erstanden*. By adopting a strict *cantus firmus* style with the melody in the bass, Lassus paid tribute to the much earlier generation of Senfl, Stoltzer, and others. The melody freely permeates the upper voices, sometimes with startling rhythmic results:

Ex. 47

The contrapuntal virtuosity is as impressive as it is concentrated (into a mere thirty bars). Other freely-composed pieces, by contrast, use a much simpler semi-chordal style with melismas on well-chosen words

---

[2] K. J. Levy, '"Susanne un jour": the History of a 16th-Century Chanson', *Annales musicologiques*, i (1953), p. 389.

[3] The German option of using instruments for some of the parts still applied.

and a melodious top part: *Wohl kombt der May*, for instance, which also illustrates the traditional *A–A–B Barform* of the German lied, originating as a medieval poetic form. The simplest approach of all is evident in the charming and justly famous *Ich weiss mir ein Meidlein*, which after the imitative *exordium* settles into the pattering rhythms and rapid-fire harmonic changes of the chanson or villanella, a manner apt for satirical words about female untrustworthiness.

Near the end of his life, Lassus published the three-part *Teutsche Psalmen* (1588) and the six-part German and French *Gesäng* (1590). The former consisted of settings of an important document of the German Counter-Reformation, the Catholic psalm translations and melodies by Caspar Ulenberg. The latter, on the other hand, included a large piece in several sections based on the Lutheran chorale *Ich ruff zu dir*, and another one set to a paraphrase of the German *Ave Maria* (*Maria voll Genad*). The leaning towards religious words is of course typical of Lassus's last years, but the interesting point is perhaps his readiness to supply music for such starkly opposed denominational needs.

CONCLUSION

LASSUS's influence upon his German contemporaries and followers was not, of course, restricted to the field of German song, even though his use of symbolism and musical imagery within that genre was profoundly significant. So ready were Lutheran church musicians to draw upon his Latin works – not only motets, but also Mass and Vespers music – that he could in some way be held responsible for preserving the Latin tradition within the Protestant rite. His Masses, Magnificats, and hymns were used without discrimination, and his motets remained a model for seventeenth-century Germans, largely through the efforts of his personal pupils, Lechner and Eccard. In other words, Lassus's 'pan-European' influence meant that his Latin music was destined for both Catholic and Protestant services, for all that this was the era of the Counter-Reformation; and Baroque Germany regarded no other sixteenth-century master as more authoritative. The attraction of this music for Lutherans is not hard to explain: the impassioned, heartfelt way Lassus approached the words he set from the Scriptures reflected the Lutheran encouragement of the individual's intimate response to the Word of God. As Blume puts it, he unlocked the meaning of the text through word-created motifs of strength and terseness.[1] Another tribute to his unassailable position of eminence after his death is that Lassus was the earliest composer in musical history whose works posterity immediately aimed to gather and preserve:[2] the result was the *Magnum opus musicum* issued by his sons in 1604 and containing the majority of the motets.

If we stand back and view Lassus's music as a whole, how did his style itself change? Much study remains to be done before a satis-factory answer can be attempted. Boetticher sees 1574 as marking the end of the 'dynamic' Lassus style; as an artist he was thereafter more 'static', bringing his own mastery to established means, and his late works were on the whole conservative.[3] We have seen how he came to favour a spiritual or ethical tone in the secular music of these late years, especially in the madrigals or chansons, and how he turned towards religious texts in the German lieder. While younger madrigalists looked to Tasso and Guarini — poets of their own generation — Lassus stuck to the poetry of Petrarch or his imitators. If change there was, it could be seen more in his tendency towards conciseness and an epigrammatic brevity of utterance, whatever the words he was setting. To say that his taste in Italian or French texts was conservative is not to suggest that he was unresponsive to changes of style in secular music. Lassus's late madrigals reveal that he was aware of the delicate contrapuntal touch and vocal 'orchestration' of Marenzio, and his lighter Italian music shows that he had noticed the rise of the new canzonetta at the expense of the cruder villanella. He flirted, momentarily, with the ideas of French *musique mesurée*. In German song, where *cantus firmus* techniques had earlier been the rule, Lassus sought flexible, illustrative motives treated freely and always preserv-ing rhetorical qualities in the music. The madrigal, the rhetorical genre *par excellence*, underpins his approach to French chanson and German lied; the latter was in any case suffering a drastic loss of

[1] F. Blume, *Protestant Church Music* (London, 1975), *passim*.
[2] Leuchtmann, op. cit., p. 187.
[3] Boetticher, op. cit., pp. 427, 699.

identity in the face of Italian influence in the later sixteenth century. Not only did Lassus strive for the rhetorical declamation of words; like many of his Continental contemporaries he turned more and more towards the vertical element in musical style. This was not so much as a direct result either of humanist principles or ecclesiastical directives (which he himself to some extent cold-shouldered), but rather because within his musical 'ego' he seems to have had a lifelong obsession with that most basic Italian chordal genre, the villanella. Its influence wells up repeatedly in his music right from the early Italian years up to his choice of models for the late Nunc dimittis settings, in his chansons and secular motets, in his feel for colourful harmony or sharply-etched, excited rhythm.

It is the international outlook unique to Lassus that called into being a bewildering number of hybrid forms and styles — the 'Latin chanson', the French villanella, the villanella-style Magnificat, the double-choir drinking song, and so on. This outlook brought to Germany a diversity of genre and musical language which wielded a tremendous influence on Lassus's pupils and admirers among the various German court composers. One could say that Lassus's cosmopolitanism was as significant for German music as Schütz's 'Italianism' was to prove several decades later. And of course Lassus's earlier friendship with both the Gabrielis on their respective visits to Munich and Venice only helped to cement musical ties between these two cities on either side of the Alps.[4]

Lassus was never a radical or progressive composer. His sacred music may have been 'madrigalized' but it never anticipated a true Baroque pathos, nor even a pre-Baroque idiom. 'Madrigalized' is the wrong word in any case; the attention he paid to the text and to its rhetorical communication place his sacred music high in the realm of liturgical art. Taking all his works together, we should acclaim Lassus as the supremely versatile cosmopolitan, the supremely prolific, famous, and influential composer of his day and, in his devotion to words, the supreme musical poet: a unique figure in musical history.

[4] See D. Arnold, *Giovanni Gabrieli* (London, 1974), pp. 10ff.

SOURCE-LIST OF WORKS
MENTIONED IN THE TEXT

Abbreviations are explained on page 57.

Title	Collected edn.	Other sources*
Motets		
Agimus tibi gratias a 3	S i, 59	Tovey LP, p. 6
Alma nemes	S iii, 93	
Alma Redemptoris II a 6	S xiii, 108	
Ave verum	S xiii, 66	Ricordi N.Y.2482; Bank gw 48
Benedic anima mea	S i, 152	Bank G 114; KSS, p. 45
Bestia curvafia pulices	H i, 67	
Cantate Domino a 3	S i, 42	KSS, p. 37
Christus resurgens	S v, 54	Chester
Cum invocarem	S xvii, 43	
Domine Deus meus	S i, 34	KSS, p. 43
Domine Jesu Christe	S v, 91	Bank gw 46
Domine quid multiplicati a 6	S xvii, 110	
Fallax gratia	S i, 143	
Fratres sobrii	S i, 129	
Fremuit spiritu Jesus	S xv, 23	Bank V 35
In convertendo	S xxi, 63	
In hora ultima	S xv, 151	Bärenreiter BA 2641
In me transierunt	S ix, 49	Bärenreiter BA 2641
In monte Oliveti	S xi, 187	
Jesu nostra redemptio	S xiii, 18	
Jubilate Deo a 4	S iii, 62	Chester M
Justorum animae	S v, 139	Chester
Lauda Sion	H i, 75	Bärenreiter BA 2915
Luxuriosa res vinum	S xv, 85	
Mirabile mysterium	S v, 18	
Missus est Gabriel	S vii, 16	
Musica Dei donum	S xix, 63	Bärenreiter BA 2642
O mors quam amara est	S xv, 67	
Omnes de Saba	S xxi, 1	
Peccantem me quotidie	S i, 159	
Prophetiae Sibyllarum		CW, xlviii; KSS, p. 81
Quasi cedrus	S i, 93	

* In this column are listed some more accessible performing editions. Publishers' serial numbers are quoted where known.

Resonet	S iii, 148	Bank K 31 (*prima pars* only)
Salve Regina II a 4	S i, 89	Chester; Bank G 8
Seven Penitential Psalms		Kalmus (published separately)
Stabunt justi	S vii, 61	
Surgens Jesus	S v, 60	
Te spectant Reginalde Poli	S iii, 127	
Tibi laus a 5	S iii, 130	
Timor et tremor	S xix, 6	CW, xiv, 6; KSS, p. 57
Tristis est anima mea	S v, 48	Bank gw 47
Tui sunt caeli	S xxi, 5	
Vexilla regis	S xi, 172	
Videntes stellam	S v, 22	Bank K 33
Vinum bonum	S xxi, 91	Arnold L, p. 58

Masses

Missa Bell'Amfitrit'altera	H viii, 55	
Missa Dixit Joseph	H viii, 3	
Missa Domine non secundum actum	H vii, 49	
Missa Doulce memoire	H iv, 3	Bärenreiter BA 4385
Missa Osculetur me	H x, 187	Bärenreiter BA 4396
Missa Pilons pilons lorge	H iii, 51	
Missa Pro defunctis a 4	H iv, 95	Bärenreiter BA 4387
Missa Pro defunctis a 5	H vi, 135	
Missa Puisque j'ay perdu	H iv, 23	Bank JL 10/12
Missa Qual donna s'attende	H vi, 43	
Missa Quand'io pens'al martire	H vii, 25	Bank JL 14
Missa Susanne un jour	H iv, 121	Bärenreiter BA 4388
Missa Triste depart	H x, 115	
Missa Vinum bonum	H v, 105	Bank JL 18/20

Other liturgical works

Lamentations of Maundy Thursday		Mapa Mundi
Magnificat Praeter rerum seriem		Mapa Mundi
Magnificat primi toni a 4 (1567)		Chester
Scio enim		Chester M
The 4 Passions	H ii	
Tenebrae Responsories of Maundy Thursday		Mapa Mundi

Madrigals and villanellas

Ben sono i premi	S vi, 137	Peters P 3506, p. 12
Cantai, or piango	S ii, 1	
Che più d'un giorno	H i, 140	
Come la notte	H i, 136	Bärenreiter BA 2913

Come lume di notte	H i, 134	
Crudele acerba	S ii, 44	
Dapoi che sotto'l ciel	H i, 172	
Deh, lascia, anima	S vi, 85	Arnold L, p. 1
Deh perchè voglio	H i, 183	
Hai Lucia	S x, 86	Arnold L, p. 37
Hor vi riconfortate	S vi, 26	Peters P 3506, p. 27
Il grave de l'età	S vi, 126	Peters P 3506, p. 5
I'vo piangendo	S iv, 116	
La cortesia	S x, 66	
La non vol esser più mia	H i, 152	
Lagrime di S. Pietro		CW, xxxiv, xxxvii, xli
Madonna mia pietà	S x, 61	CW, viii, 22
Madonna sa l'amor	H i, 156	
Matona mia cara	S x, 93	Peters P 3506, p. 37
O la, o che bon eccho	S x, 140	Peters P 3506, p. 41
O occhi manza mia	S x, 103	Penguin M, p. 130
Occhi piangete	S viii, 19	CW, xiii, 4; Arnold L, p. 24
Ove le luci giro	H i, 163	
Passan vostri trionfi	S x, 53	Peters P 4812
Per aspro mar	S vi, 70	
Quanto il mio duol	S viii, 31	Penguin M, p. 124
Queste non son più lagrime	S viii, 15	Arnold L, p. 27
Solo e pensoso	S ii, 71	Arnold L, p. 5
Sotto quel sta	S viii, 76	Arnold L, p. 32
Spesso in poveri alberghi	S viii, 83	CW, xiii, 7

Chansons

Bon jour mon coeur	S xii, 100	HAM, i, 159; LPM, p. 14
En espoir vis	S xii, 52	
En un chasteau	S xii, 14	
Fleur de quinze ans	S xii, 43	
Heureux qui met		JAMS, xxvii (1974), 322
Je l'ayme bien	S xii, 41	CW, xiii, 5
Je suis quasi prest d'enrager	S xii, 54	
La nuict froide et sombre	S xii, 34	CW, xiii, 9
Las voulez-vous	S xii, 3	
Mais qui pourroit a 3	S xvi, 107	Bank gp 20
Margot labourez les vignes	S xii, 102	LPM, p. 12
Monsieur l'abbé	S xii, 16	
O foible esprit	S xvi, 34	CW, xiii, 17
Quand mon mari	S xii, 23	LPM, p. 16
Qui dort icy?	S xii, 19	
Si du malheur	S xii, 30	
Soyons joyeux	S xii, 20	LPM, p. 20
Susanne un jour	S xiv, 29	IM, vi, 10
Un jour vis un foulon	S xii, 39	
Une puce	S xiv, 114	
Vray Dieu disoit une fillette	S xii, 72	

Lieder

Audite nova! Der Bau'r	S xx, 51	AC, ii, 142
Christ ist erstanden	S xx, 3	AC, i, 140
Ein guter Wein	S xviii, 44	AC, ii, 130
Es jagt ein Jäger	S xviii, 88	AC, ii, 132
Ich ruff zu dir	S xx, 88	
Ich weiss mir ein Meidlein	S xx, 28	AC, ii, 140; KSS, p. 105
Maria voll Genad	S xx, 108	AC, i, 132
Susannen frumb	S xviii, 109	
Vater unser	S xviii, 1	
Wohl kombt der May	S xx, 40	AC, ii, 129

ABBREVIATIONS

Collected edition

S   *R. de Lassus: Sämtliche Werke*, ed. F. X. Haberl and A. Sandberger (Leipzig, 1894-1926)

H   *R. de Lassus: Sämtliche Werke: Neue Reihe*, ed. S. Hermelink and others (Kassel, 1956–)

Other sources

AC	*Antiqua Chorbuch*, ed. H. Mönkemeyer (Mainz, 1951-2)
Arnold L	*Orlandus Lassus: Ten Madrigals*, ed. D. Arnold (London, 1977)
Chester M	*The Fifth Book of Chester Motets*, ed. A. G. Petti (London, 1977)
CW	*Das Chorwerk*, various editors (Wolfenbüttel, 1929–)
HAM	A. Davison and W. Apel, *Historical Anthology of Music*, 1946
IM	*Invitation to Madrigals*, vi, ed. D. Scott (London, 1973)
JAMS	*Journal of the American Musicological Society*
KSS	Kalmus Study Score No. 707, 1968
LPM	London Pro Musica Edition, *Anthologies of Renaissance Music*, i (London, 1977)
Penguin M	*The Penguin Book of Italian Madrigals*, ed. J. Roche (London, 1974)
Tovey LP	*Laudate Pueri*, ed. D. F. Tovey (London, 1910)

SELECT BIBLIOGRAPHY

D. ARNOLD, 'The Grand Motets of Orlandus Lassus', *Early Music*, vi (1978), pp. 170-81.

J. BERNSTEIN, 'Lassus in English Sources: Two Chansons Recovered', *Journal of the American Musicological Society*, xxvii (1974), pp. 315-25.

F. BLUME, *Protestant Church Music* (London, 1975).

W. BOETTICHER, *Orlando di Lasso und sein Zeit, 1532-1594* (Kassel, 1958).

—— 'Anticipations of Dramatic Monody in the Late Works of Lassus', *Essays on Opera and English Music*, ed. F. W. Sternfeld and others (Oxford, 1975), pp. 84-102.

A. EINSTEIN, *The Italian Madrigal* (Princeton, 1949, repr. 1971), pp. 477 ff.

J. HAAR, 'A madrigal falsely ascribed to Lasso', *Journal of the American Musicological Society*, xxviii (1975), pp. 526-9.

—— 'Lassus', *The New Grove Dictionary of Music and Musicians* (London, 1980).

H. LEUCHTMANN, *Orlando di Lasso* (2 vols.: I. *Leben*; II. *Briefe*) (Wiesbaden, 1976-7).

K. LEVY, '"Susanne un jour": The History of a 16th-Century Chanson', *Annales musicologiques*, i (1953), pp. 375-408.

E. LOWINSKY, 'The musical avant-garde of the Renaissance, or the peril and profit of foresight', in *Art, Science, and History in the Renaissance*, ed. C. S. Singleton (Baltimore, 1967), pp. 11-162.

W. MITCHELL, 'The prologue to Orlando di Lasso's Prophetiae Sibyllarum', *Music Forum*, ii (1970), pp. 264-73.

C. PALISCA, 'Ut oratoria musica: the rhetorical basis of musical mannerism', *The Meaning of Mannerism*, ed. F. W. Robinson and S. G. Nichols (Hanover, N.H., 1972), p. 37.

R. HINTON THOMAS, *Poetry and Song in the German Baroque* (Oxford, 1963).